Customer Retention
in a week

JANE SMITH

Hodder & Stoughton

A MEMBER OF THE HODDER HEADLINE GROUP

Orders: please contact Bookpoint Ltd, 130 Milton Park, Abingdon, Oxon
OX14 4SB.
Telephone: (44) 01235 827720, Fax: (44) 01235 400454. Lines are open from
9.00–6.00, Monday to Saturday, with a 24 hour message answering service.
Email address: orders@bookpoint.co.uk

British Library Cataloguing in Publication Data
A catalogue record for this title is available from The British Library

ISBN 0 340 84938 X

First published	2000
Impression number	10 9 8 7 6 5 4 3 2 1
Year	2007 2006 2005 2004 2003 2002

Typeset by SX Composing DTP, Rayleigh, Essex.
Printed in Great Britain for Hodder & Stoughton Educational, a division of
Hodder Headline Plc, 338 Euston Road, London NW1 3BH by
Cox & Wyman Ltd, Reading, Berkshire.

The leading organisation for professional management

As the champion of management, the Chartered Management Institute shapes and supports the managers of tomorrow. By sharing intelligent insights and setting standards in management development, the Institute helps to deliver results in a dynamic world.

Setting and raising standards

The Institute is a nationally accredited organisation, responsible for setting standards in management and recognising excellence through the award of professional qualifications.

Encouraging development, improving performance

The Institute has a vast range of development programmes, qualifications, information resources and career guidance to help managers and their organisations meet new challenges in a fast-changing environment.

Shaping opinion

With in-depth research and regular policy surveys of its 91,000 individual members and 520 corporate members, the Chartered Management Institute has a deep understanding of the key issues. Its view is informed, intelligent and respected.

For more information call 01536 204222 or visit www.managers.org.uk

CONTENTS

■ I N T R O D U C T I O N ■

To survive and prosper in today's tough business environment, everything we do has to be focused on the needs of our customers. Easy to say but hard to do. Competition is so strong that if people don't get what they want from us, they will buy elsewhere. But it is not enough to attract customers once and then to allow them to drift away – the key to success is to make them feel so satisfied that they will want to remain loyal forever.

Our customers are better informed and have higher expectations than ever before – and the range of choices open to them in the global marketplace is wider than at any time in the history of commerce. To attract enough of these customers and, once we have them, to retain them, we have to work hard to please them. If we can do this better than our competitors – not just once but at every transaction – our customers will keep coming back.

This book explores some basic principles of customer retention. We discuss why it's important to identify customers and their needs and how we can give these customers exactly what they want, every time. The book contains some tried and tested customer retention tools and techniques as well as a number of hints and tips on how to make sure both staff and customers feel recognised and valued.

Why is it important to retain customers?

We are going to start the week by looking at why 'customer retention' has recently become one of the hottest topics for discussion in business circles. Suddenly the buzz words are 'customer loyalty', 'customer focus', 'delighting the customer' and 'relationship marketing'. The reason for this new obsession is simple – improving customer retention pays big dividends. Studies have shown that increasing customer retention by just 5% can have a bottom line profit increase of up to 75%. And the 'lifetime value' of a single customer can be measured in many thousands of pounds, depending on the type of business. We cannot escape from the simple fact that retaining customers, satisfying them and making them enthusiastic champions of our products are vital – not just to business success, but to business survival.

Focusing on customers, not products

Retaining customers means spending less time looking for new customers and more time looking after the ones we already have, so that they will grow into bigger customers. Tom Peters said it all during the 1980s in his book *Thriving on Chaos* – and his words are even more true today. His argument was that every customer should be considered both as an appreciating asset and as a powerful tool for word-of-mouth advertising.

'It boils down to this: When you build a plant, it starts depreciating the day it opens. The well-served customer, on the other hand, is an

*appreciating asset. Every small act on her or his behalf ups the odds
for repeat business, add-on business and priceless word-of-mouth
referral.'*

To retain customers, it is vital to focus on what people want
and need, rather than on what we want to sell to them. For
many years, organisations tended to be very inward looking.
They were primarily concerned about the quality of the
goods they produced or the services they provided. They
worried endlessly about devising the most efficient systems
and procedures; they debated the benefits and problems of
different production methods and they spent a lot of time
considering how best to sell those goods and services to
people out there in the marketplace. 'Customer service' –
when it existed – was frequently an 'extra' that was bolted on
at the end of the production line.

In recent times, however, all that has changed. Customers
have become more knowledgeable and more demanding
than ever before – and they have far more choice about what

and where they should buy. This means that, even though an organisation may be producing the best product or offering the most efficient service in the world, it will not be successful unless it bends all its efforts towards finding out what customers want and then offering this to them. To retain customers you have to base *everything* that you do on the needs, wants and expectations of customers. In the words of a Ford Motor executive:

'If we are not customer driven, our cars won't be either'.

But these ideas haven't suddenly arrived like a bolt from the blue – business gurus and strategists have been talking for years about the need to get closer to the customer. The difference now, however, is that we can no longer afford to pay mere lip service to the idea. Customers' instant access to information from around the world about competing products or services – and about others' opinions on those products or services – has sounded the death knell of the cosy, long-term client relationship.

You are a customer too

Do you need any more convincing of the need to bend all your efforts to listening to customers? If so, you only have to think about the times when you have been a customer – in shops or restaurants, with insurance companies, gas and electricity providers, and so on. What are the best and the worst examples of customer service **you** have ever experienced?

Like every one of us, it is most likely that you have had pleasant encounters similar to this . . .

'*After two days travelling, I emerged tired and totally disorientated into the arrivals lounge at Sydney. To my relief and delight I spotted someone holding a sign with my name on it. He smiled, took my bags and led me to a waiting taxi. At my hotel a willing attendant opened the door and the receptionist welcomed me warmly by name.*'

. . . and this . . .

'*Although he was obviously busy, the waiter came up to us immediately and greeted us as he offered us the menus and took our drinks order. The drinks came within five minutes together with a selection of things to nibble – this was great because we were feeling quite hungry*'.

Unfortunately, it's almost certain that you can also remember unpleasant ones, like this . . .

'*On the way to work this morning I bought breakfast from a sandwich bar near the station. The assistant was rather unshaven and short tempered. His wake up call to each to each customer, including myself, was a sudden snarled 'Yeah?' as he jabbed the air with his chin*'.

. . . and this . . .

'*I couldn't believe the way that shop assistant behaved! She managed to complete an entire credit card transaction with me just now while talking on a mobile phone!*'

It's not hard to guess which of the above customers will remain loyal to their respective suppliers and which will go elsewhere at the earliest opportunity. The great thing is that each one of these good and bad examples of customer service holds valuable lessons for all of us. As customers, we are usually satisfied when:

- Services and products are designed with customers' real needs in mind
- Products and services exceed our expectations in some way
- We are treated as individuals – not as just the next customer in the line
- Our complaints are dealt with efficiently and sympathetically
- People working for the supplier have a friendly and helpful attitude
- They have the authority to make decisions and show initiative when solving our problems.

The main aim of this book is to give you a clear idea of what you can do to achieve these points.

Why have things changed?

There are two main reasons why, in order to retain customers, it is now necessary to concern ourselves primarily with their needs, rather than with the services or products we offer:

> 1 The external environment has changed
> 2 Customers themselves have changed.

The business environment
Business organisations in the 21st century operate in a world of uncertainty, complexity and rapid change. You are probably well aware of the main factors that have brought this situation about:

- **Intensifying competition**: all organisations are to a greater or lesser extent influenced and affected by the global competitive environment. But as competition intensifies, our ability to retain customers is the most important way of gaining the competitive edge.

- **Rapid technological innovation**: new information systems, the internet and intranet technologies have created new business possibilities, including methods of carrying out transactions and communicating with colleagues and customers. These technological advances have revolutionised the way many of us do business, they have helped to improve general efficiency and have often resulted in substantial cost savings.

- **Constant demand for higher quality and better value**: in the face of increasing competition, it's no good striving for quality and then sitting back once we have achieved it. Instead, we have to work *continuously* to improve the quality of the service we provide for our customers.

Succeeding in the competitive environment means never losing our awareness of changing customer needs. This involves:

* Recognising and managing changes before they take control of us, and
* Developing our skills, our organisational structures and our business processes in such a way that we can easily turn the threat of change into an opportunity for growth.

Customers
In general terms, individual customers are today better educated and better informed than their parents or grandparents. They are aware of their legal and moral rights and they take time to find out about the products that are available and to compare features and prices.

Added to this, customers have personal dreams and aspirations which go far beyond the modest expectations of previous generations. They are less likely to accept unquestioningly their situation in the world; they are often motivated by a need to improve their physical circumstances and to realise their desire for self-fulfilment.

In addition, it has become more and more common for customers to own shares in the organisations that serve them. Those that do have an extra stake have a further incentive to take an interest in that organisation's overall performance.

Although the consequences of ignoring the demands and expectations of customers can be severe for businesses, it would be wrong to view these new attitudes and needs as a problem. On the contrary, we can gain distinct competitive advantage if we recognise and meet the characteristics of the

new consumer. Increasingly, what is important for them is not what they are buying, but how they are treated by the organisation doing the selling.

The benefits of retaining customers

Retaining customers is not only in the best interests of the organisation: customers also benefit from creating long-term partnerships with the people who provide them with goods and services.

Benefits for customers
Despite the volatility and lack of barriers in modern marketplaces, many customers still have a natural preference for remaining with suppliers who understand their needs and their preferences. This is because they are aware of the time and effort involved in searching for a new supplier each time they want to make a purchase. Once customers have taken the time to educate their providers, and are getting what they want, they can start to relax because they know they can rely on a consistent level of quality service.

In certain cases, a supplier may even become part of a customer's social support system. Good examples of this are:

- A hairdresser or barman who serves as a personal confidant
- The proprietor of a village post office who is a central figure in neighbourhood activities
- The doctor who knows an entire family and its special needs
- The cleaner who becomes a close family friend and can be called upon to look after children, walk the dog, water the plants and feed the cat when the need arises.

The benefits which arise from these types of close personal relationships (which can develop for both business and private customers) are important ingredients of a customer's quality of life and will add incalculable value to the immediate benefits of the actual service provided.

Benefits for the organisation
Developing a loyal customer base brings many benefits for the organisation – most of them directly linked to the bottom line. The main ones are:

- **Increased sales**: as customers get to know your firm and are content with what they are getting, they will start to give you more business. As time passes, they may want more of what you are offering. This is why, if you develop new products and services over the years, it is a good idea to offer them first to existing, satisfied customers rather than to scramble for new ones

- **Lower costs**: this is the 'leaky bucket' syndrome. It costs far more to keep topping up the bucket with new customers than to stop existing customers from leaking away by plugging the hole at the bottom. When you are calculating the cost of finding new customers, it's not just the advertising costs that you need to take into account. There is also the time it takes to find out about new customers' needs and answer their questions. Few of these initial costs can be recouped from the revenue that flows in from new customers – but they will become negligible if they can be spread over several transactions and a number of years.

- **Word of mouth advertising**: in today's overcrowded and complex marketplace customers often ask friends, colleagues and family members to recommend products or service providers. Positive word-of-mouth advertising from satisfied, loyal customers is both the cheapest (it's free!) and the most effective advertising that you can use – whether you are selling to business customers or to private individuals.

- **Employee retention**: employees like to work for companies whose customers are happy and loyal because this makes their jobs more satisfying. It follows that employees stay longer in those organisations which have a loyal customer base. As a result, service quality improves and costs of staff turnover are reduced, all of which adds further to profits.

The argument for focusing efforts on retaining customers rather than on looking for new ones can be supported by looking at the concept of the 'lifetime value of a customer'.

One very successful minimarket owner-manager in a Sussex village calculated the potential lifetime value of a single one of his customers at £25,000. He arrived at this figure by multiplying an average £50.00 per week (£2,500 a year) grocery bill by an estimated life span as a customer of 10 years.

Try a similar calculation for your customers – you may be surprised by the revenue that each one contributes, as well as by the profits you stand to lose when one defects to the competition.

Creating long-term relationships

If you succeed in creating good long-term partnerships with customers, you stand a good chance of building up trust and breaking down the barriers between you. Creating a partnership involves developing a shared vision of what you are both aiming to achieve and then working to build a relationship in which there is a free exchange of information, honesty, mutual respect and, most important of all, a lasting commitment on both sides.

Even if your customer doesn't yet trust you enough to see you as this kind of partner, this is a worthwhile goal to work towards. Show that you are loyal to customers and genuinely have their best interests at heart. If you can do this, there's a good chance that they will return that loyalty by seeing you as a reliable, effective, long-term partner.

Putting your customers first

Retaining customers involves getting a clear idea of what their requirements are, delivering these requirements and then responding quickly when they change (as they inevitably will). This means that your core activity must be satisfying customers rather than producing particular goods or services. If you do this, your organisation will be 'customer-driven' rather than 'supply-led'.

Although delighting the customer looks simple on paper, it can be a real challenge to say to customers 'I want you to tell me what you think' – and then to act quickly and willingly on the feedback. A growing mountain of evidence must, however, convince you that the companies which survive and thrive in the competitive global marketplace are the ones that are willing to listen, to learn and to act.

But before you can identify people's exact requirements, you first have to get to know your customers better. In fact, you have to know them better than they know themselves so that you can identify what they need now and anticipate what they may require in the future. This may not be easy, because 'customers' are a complex group, and in order to guarantee prosperity you have to identify them all and satisfy them all.

Who are your customers?

We all know who customers are – they're the people and organisations who buy the products and services we produce. And of course, this is true: the people who actually put their hands in their pockets are the most important people to focus on, because without them our businesses would not survive. However, there is a whole range of other people, departments and organisations that we also need to see as customers – because their expectations and requirements must be satisfied if the final, external customer is to be satisfied. In fact, the term 'customers' has been defined by some commentators as anyone whose decisions can determine whether or not an organisation will prosper.

The success of most businesses depends on their ability to maintain the loyalty of several different customer groups:

- **Consumers**: these are the people or organisations who use the products you produce – and they may or may not be the ones who actually pay for them. For example the consumer of a toy is a child but the purchaser is usually an adult; the consumer of medical supplies is a patient but the purchaser is often a hospital or GP's surgery.

- **Purchasers**: these are the people or organisations who actually pay for your products or services. They could be members of the general public or other businesses. Purchasers can also include distributors or dealers who make your products and services available to final customers. These are sometimes called 'intermediate customers'.

- **Internal customers**: these are the people or teams within the organisation who process work on the way to serving intermediate or final customers. Most people inside an organisation pass their work on to others after they have finished with it. In manufacturing, people on an assembly line are suppliers and customers to each other; in a managerial context, a manager's internal customers may be team members, colleagues, administrative staff and managers further up the organisational hierarchy.

- **Suppliers**: to gear up your business to deliver satisfaction for customers, it is vital to create close alliances with your suppliers. These are the people or organisations who supply you with the resources and raw materials that are processed into the product that is delivered to your final customer.

These different groups of customers link up in what is known as the 'customer – supplier chain' or 'supply chain', every aspect of which must work efficiently if you are to retain customers.

To get an idea of how the supply chain works, think what happens when a lump of iron is transformed into an engine block in a foundry. When the process is complete, the engine block is worth more than the iron it is made from – value has been added to it by the production processes. It's not quite so obvious in other types of businesses, but the basic principle is the same. Value is added to the goods and services that we provide for customers as they pass along the customer-supplier chain, and this added value is what our customers pay for.

Although it is important to identify your internal customers and their needs, these individuals and groups are not customers in quite the same sense as end users. The essential difference is that end users can go elsewhere if they choose to do so, whereas internal customers have no such choice. External and internal customers are similar, however, in that both have requirements which must be identified and met. Failing to meet the needs of internal customers leads to inefficiencies in the process, which in turn ultimately results in failing to provide satisfaction for end users.

Fitting into the big picture

An organisation can only beat off competition, keep existing customers and win new ones if it can manage every part of the supply chain to optimum effect. Everyone within the chain needs to understand who their own customers are and then to fulfil each of these customers' requirements. Adopting this perspective, in which no one sees their work as an isolated function but recognises it as a vital element of the greater operation, may require a significant change in the culture of some organisations.

One of the UK's largest companies takes the concept of the internal customer so seriously that it has drawn up a complete set of standards which define every aspect of the way in which work is handed from one department to the next on its way to the final customer.

If you are a manager, communicating the customer-centred message to members of your team is one of your most important tasks. Studies show that people are unlikely to be motivated if they don't understand the purpose of what they are doing and who it is for. So all of your team members need to know who their customers are, how they fit into the big picture and how their own work contributes to delivering products and services to final customers and end users.

The customer's perspective

Taking this wider view and seeing each individual operation as just one part of the supply chain may or may not involve a new perspective for people within the organisation. But for the external customer, the perspective is completely different. Your customers are buying a particular service or a product, and have no interest in how the operation is sliced up.

One of the best illustrations of what happens when businesses fail to see things from the end user's point of view can be found in the rail industry. The various rail businesses continue to remain blind to the fact that commuters have absolutely no interest in apportioning blame when the system fails to deliver the promised standards of service. In fact, many commentators believe that the attempts by Railtrack and the individual train operators to blame each other for shortfalls in performance has done more than anything else to create the current public relations disaster.

To be sure of retaining customers, you need to be able to see what you are offering through their eyes – as one integrated operation. What this means in practice is being aware that if one of the processes within the supply chain fails in some way, then so does the process as a whole. The result is that you fail your customers.

Unfortunately, businesses tend only to get feedback from customers when things go wrong. Although it may be unpleasant to hear this type of information, it is also

extremely valuable because once we know where the problems are, we can start to put them right.

The key point to remember is that the success or failure of the supply chain is everyone's responsibility. Although a problem that gives rise to a complaint may not have been caused by your team, the final customer is only concerned about the overall failure to provide the product or service they have paid for and expect to receive.

Solving problems
One way of helping members of your team to see things from a customer's perspective is to get them involved in spotting problems and identifying how these can be solved. As we have seen, this means getting them to look at the operation as a whole – not just at their own part of it. And don't just look for problems – get people to look at areas where things are already working well but could be improved. Team members are the people who know the job best and, as they often have

the most contact with the final customer, tremendous benefits can be gained from securing their involvement. This course of action also breaks down barriers between the different parts of the supply chain and makes individuals more prepared to take responsibility for putting things right.

Profiling your customers

Once you know who your customers are and where they fit in the customer-supply chain, the next step is to get to know them better. This can be a very time-consuming process, but it does not have to be done quickly. Knowing even a small amount about your customers will pay dividends in the end. As you collect information about your customers (or more likely your customer groups) you can start to draw up a profile of their characteristics. This information will enable you to tailor your whole approach to retaining these customers.

As an example, here is a profile of the preferred customers of a credit card issuer

- They earn more than £40,000 per year
- They are home owners
- They are car owners
- They are over 35
- They are frequent internet users
- They go abroad on holiday at least once a year
- They have been employed continuously for at least 15 years
- They have a 10-year history of paying their bills on time.

> Armed with this profile, the organisation was able to better target its marketing efforts and then 'mass customise' its products and services to the requirements of its target customers.

Building up a profile of customers and their characteristics will ensure that your services and products take account of any special needs or interests which the group may have. You will then be able to keep a picture of a 'typical' customer in mind and make sure that everything you do is geared towards meeting those needs.

Your customer groups for particular products or services may consist of private individuals or of organisations.

Individual profiles
The key characteristics you identify for individuals may include:

- Age group
- Sex
- Education/qualifications
- Income bracket
- Assets
- Personal goals
- What interests or motivates them.

Business profiles
The key characteristics you identify for business customers may include:

- Type of industry or sector
- Number of employees

- Where located
- How the business is structured
- Main activities and outputs
- Annual turnover
- Annual profit
- Business aims
- Values.

Internal customer profiles
If you do not have any contact with end users/external customers, you may find it more useful to draw up a profile of your internal customers. This will again help you to determine their needs and wants and how best you can serve them.

Collecting information about customers
Even if you already know something about your customer groups, it is wise to keep your information up to date and to keep checking that your assumptions about them are still valid. Markets move fast, and you can't afford to be unaware of customers' changing needs. There are many ways in which you and your team can collect information about customers, including:

- Talking and listening to them
- Sending out questionnaires
- Reading marketing information or company reports
- Looking at their websites
- Focus groups.

The profiles you draw up from the information you collect will help you to understand:

- How you can best retain existing customers

- Which customers you ought to be targeting for a specific product or service that you offer
- Which customers you ought **not** to be targeting.

The advantage of having plenty of relevant up to date information is that you can start to choose your customers, rather than cast your net too widely. Many businesses have prospered because they have been able to select the customers on which they should focus. Some hotels, for example, set their focus clearly on business customers rather than families on holiday. And magazines and clothes shops target their customers groups by characteristics such as age, sex and income group.

You will have chosen your customers wisely if:

1 They have needs you can meet
2 Your organisation has the resources to meet those needs both now and in the future
3 You can meet those customers' needs better than the competition
4 They are able to pay you properly for meeting their needs.

What do your customers want?

We have seen that all too often organisations are only concerned about their goods and services from the point of view of producing or providing them. But the days of Henry Ford offering customers the Model T 'in any colour as long as it is black' have long gone. Now, the only route to success is to devise ways of getting close to customers, of listening to what they want and then offering this to them.

In today's chapter you are going to look at the kinds of things that our customers expect, how you might collect information about your customers' needs and how you can measure the extent to which you are meeting those needs.

Keeping customers satisfied

Here's a true story . . .

A friend of a friend wanted to fix up some shelves in the kitchen. As he was unused to DIY, he decided to go to a store which he had visited before, where he remembered the staff had been particularly helpful. It wasn't hard to find the right section inside the store, but selecting the right materials was another matter entirely as the choice was completely overwhelming. Rather than make a costly mistake, he decided to ask someone for advice. He spent the next few minutes searching, and eventually found a rather scruffy looking assistant lurking behind a stack of garden furniture. When asked which materials would be best for the job

> in hand, the assistant looked completely blank, said abruptly, 'That's not my department,' and scurried away into the warehouse. Just before he disappeared the friend caught sight of the assistant's badge. It said 'I'm Steve, I'm here to help'.
>
> The friend left the store immediately, promising himself that he would never use that store, or any others in the same chain again.

This story illustrates the trap that many companies fall into. Too many launch a costly and ambitious 'customer first' campaign with all the associated mission statements, published values, staff training, customer charters, posters and badges – and then completely fail to ensure that the values actually enter the company culture.

The things that customers want

Researchers have identified a number of factors that seem to influence customers' decisions to remain loyal. They have found out that customers will usually come back if:

- You keep your promises
- You are willing to help
- You inspire confidence
- You treat customers as individuals
- You make it easy for customers to do business with you

- All the physical aspects of your product or service give a favourable impression.

Keeping promises

Most customers rate reliability as the most important factor that influences their loyalty. You are highly likely to retain customers if they believe you are dependable, if the product or service you provide is of the expected quality and if you deliver it by the agreed deadline.

Of course, mistakes and problems will sometimes occur, even in businesses which are efficiently organised and managed. Most customers will forgive you for these if you have an effective system for resolving problems or rectifying mistakes. Although dependability may be taken for granted in some cases, you can be sure that any failures which are not adequately resolved will not only be remembered but will almost certainly result in negative referrals to other potential customers.

Because the need for reliability is so important for customers, many companies have identified 'doing it right first time' as an important objective. However 'doing it right first time' means different things to different customers and you need to check carefully what customers want (what they perceive as 'right') before setting your manufacturing or service delivery standards. We look at ways of checking their exact requirements later in this section.

Being willing to help

This factor is about the willingness of the organisation and its employees to respond quickly to customers' requests and problems. On the whole, customers will remain loyal if they can see that people listen and respond promptly to their needs. Again, the customer's opinion about how willingness should be defined is more important than that of the business.

In many service companies, staff are now encouraged to create opportunities to delight the customer by over-delivering on promises.

In one building society, members of the customer service team promise to phone back within 48 hours, but in fact always aim to call back sooner than this.

Another example is the internal motto of an insurance company which is 'Say yes, not no'. Although up to 20% of calls asking for a motor insurance quote are deemed too high a risk by the company's computer system, staff are empowered to query this, to look further and to try to find a valid reason for saying 'yes'.

Inspiring confidence

> The Chief Executive of a hi-tech pioneer remote
> banking service said: 'Our customers don't want to buy
> banking services. They want to feel good, they want
> reassurance that they are in control'.

The ability to make customers trust the organisation and
have confidence in it is a critical factor in building customer
loyalty. It is particularly important for banks and other
financial services organisations to inspire confidence – but
most other organisations will find it useful to set standards
under this heading too.

You can inspire confidence in a number of ways:

- By demonstrating knowledge about your products and
  services
- By showing respect and consideration for customers
- By communicating effectively with customers – using
  language that they can understand.

All employees need to have a good product knowledge – not
just those whose primary role is to sell to customers. People
from all parts and all levels of the organisation can play their
part in telling customers about products and services and
building up a picture which inspires customers with
confidence. Van drivers, shelf stackers, administrative staff,
receptionists, waiters and staff in the support services should
all see it as part of their role to be proactive in marketing and
promoting the organisation and its products.

Treating customers as individuals

Acting spontaneously in response to customers' needs and showing that the organisation cares about them as individuals are other vital elements of maintaining loyalty. As well being able to make decisions and take responsibility, this means that employees need to empathise with customers and to build up personal relationships with them.

You might think that treating customers as individuals is only possible for small or medium sized organisations. But technology now enables even very large organisations to do this.

> The Chief Executive of a global financial services organisation said, 'Customers want to be known as an individual. And when they call us again they can pick up where they left off. It's as if the 4,000 of us are one'.

Making it easy

Many companies have thrived simply because they have understood and acted on customers' need for easy or convenient access to or delivery of their products and services. If the customers who are likely to want what you offer are at work between 9am and 5pm, it doesn't make any sense to shut up your own shop at the same time. In some types of business, customers who are short of time now want to be able to trade at almost any hour of the day.

This again involves trying to see your business from the customer's point of view, and then working out what could be making it difficult for them to purchase from you.

A car dealer realised that its location on an out-of-town retail park was making it hard for customers to leave their cars for servicing. Things quickly looked up when the company introduced a range of solutions which included courtesy cars, transport to the city centre using the neighbouring supermarket's free bus service or, for a small extra charge, picking up the customer's car from his or her workplace/home and redelivering it once the servicing had been carried out.

Another company looked at the stockbroking marketplace and concluded: 'Historically it had been very complex – dominated by men in stripy suits and not everyone feels comfortable with that. There seemed to be a lot of hoops to jump through and the whole experience of sharedealing seemed pretty intimidating and very expensive. We set out to create a service where it was easy to register'.

E-companies are particularly well placed to offer simplicity and convenience.

One online book store provides a free service where, if you buy a book as a gift, the company emails a greeting to the recipient telling him or her the title of the book, with the gift itself arriving, suitably packaged, a day or two later. This service has the added advantage of allowing the book store to introduce itself to yet another potential customer.

Giving the right impression

Nearly everything that you do makes an impression on a potential or current customer. Are your premises clean and safe? Is your equipment organised neatly? Is the outside of your building as attractive as possible? Does your letterhead or annual report project an appropriate image? Experts say that strong first impressions are created during the first 30 seconds of any encounter – this means that we may never get the chance to put right the consequences of a bad start. It is therefore crucial to make sure that everything the customer sees projects the right image, including the appearance of:

- The people who work in the company
- Your business premises
- Company cars and other vehicles
- Stationery
- Any documents that will be read by external or internal customers.

Things like premises are, of course, of even greater significance when customers have to go there to purchase or use the product or service you are offering.

Creating customer-defined standards

Knowing the kinds of characteristics that are important to your customers is only the first step. The really important bit is finding out exactly what your customers want and what level of performance you have to achieve on each characteristic to satisfy them. Once this has been done, you can design a system to measure how well you are meeting their needs week by week and month by month.

First, you need a list of the characteristics that you think may be important to your customers, and the factors described earlier in this chapter are a good place to start. You can then refine and add to this list by using one or more of a whole range of techniques, including:

- **Sending out a questionnaire**: this is a time-honoured method of information gathering, but to be useful they have to be professionally produced and, even then, response levels are often low.

- **Organising a focus group**: you can glean a lot of information by inviting a small group of customers to meet you to answer questions on their needs, their problems and their expectations. In a meeting, you can pursue a particular line of enquiry and observe people's body language as well as listen to their verbal answers and reactions.

- **Visiting customers**: you can learn a lot about people's requirements by visiting customers on their own premises. Actually hearing and seeing customers is often the best way to identify problems and individual requirements.

- **Telephoning customers**: information on needs and required levels of performance can be gathered quickly and easily in a telephone call.

- **Experiencing the product or service first hand**: to appreciate what customers want and need it's always valuable to experience your products and services from the receiving end. Find out (first hand) what it's like to be a customer in your shop, to assemble one of your flatpack chests of drawers, to be a passenger on one of your buses, to eat a meal in your restaurant or to book seats in your theatre. If you are a senior executive, it may be best to go incognito, or at least arrive unannounced, otherwise you will be given special treatment.

- **'Mystery shoppers'**: these are used in situations where it is difficult for managers to gather enough of this type of information for themselves.

All these approaches will enable you to get closer to your customers – and when you can do that you are more likely to give them what they want and gain valuable competitive advantage. Don't forget that these methods can also help you to gain information about internal customers.

The next challenge is to translate the information you gather into clearly defined standards. This means that customers themselves define the quality of service they expect and require when they deal with your business. It's important to make these standards measurable, so that you can keep a constant check on how well you are doing.

Here are some examples of customer-defined standards:

- Deliver the correct orders on or before the promised date
- Produce goods of the required quality at the agreed time
- Process instructions by an agreed deadline
- Install equipment correctly and within a defined timeframe
- Use customers' names when talking to them.

Your standard could also include a target to aim for, so that you can measure how consistently you are providing customers with what they want. For example:

- Return calls the same day for at least 97% of customers
- Resolve problems within 24 hours for at least 98% of customers
- Serve at least 95% of customers within five minutes.

Of course, there is little point in going to the trouble of finding out what customers want and setting standards if you don't communicate this information to the entire workforce. You should never assume that people already know what customers need. Even a little information can make a huge difference to people's performance – and the result is often that customers are truly delighted.

Again, remember that products and services and customer groups and their needs are constantly changing. The process of finding out what customers want is not something that you do once and then forget – you have to check constantly on what customers want and that you are still giving them what they want. To be sure of success this process should be established as a matter of routine.

Measuring your success

Living up to customer-defined standards is not easy – it is not enough to meet them in certain parts of the company or on certain days of the year. To keep customers coming back, everyone has to meet these standards for every customer every time they come to purchase. Only if you can do this can you say that you are truly providing customer satisfaction.

The only way of making sure that your organisation is meeting your customer-defined standards is to introduce reliable measurement systems. The method you select will depend on the types of standards that you have defined. Measurement is easier for certain characteristics than for others. In some cases, it is possible to judge the quality of products and services purely by keeping count. For example:

- The number of errors made (bank)
- The number of goods produced (manufacturer)
- The number of visits made (health visitor)
- Amount of food left on a plate (restaurant).

However, with many other characteristics the only way of measuring the extent to which standards are being achieved is to seek customers' opinions directly. The usual ways of doing this are customer feedback forms, postal surveys and customer interviews. As it is expensive to collect measurement information, you should measure only what you need to know. The questions you ask must be designed to elicit information on only the characteristics you have already identified – the standards that you know you must meet to maintain the loyalty of your customers.

Feedback forms
Reactionnaires or comment cards are a valuable way of measuring satisfaction because they provide you with instant feedback on your successes and problem areas. It is only possible to collect feedback in this way if you come into direct contact with your customers. You can often find examples in hotels, restaurants, banks, health clubs, retail outlets or transport services.

The main pitfall is that you will only get feedback from people who are motivated to provide it for some reason.

Their responses may, therefore, not be typical. Because of this, companies frequently provide some sort of incentive for people who complete questionnaires – usually a free gift or the chance to enter a competition. The more attractive the prize, the more motivated customers will be to complete the feedback form.

Postal surveys
This method is used by all types of business – especially those that never or rarely come into contact with their customers. Postal surveys are more expensive to organise than instant feedback forms or comment cards, but most customers are likely to appreciate the opportunity to provide an opinion on your product or service. Again, you will usually get more responses if you make it easy for people to reply and offer some form of reward.

Interviews
If they are properly structured, customer interviews can be an effective method of probing 'real' information, as you can follow up and clarify any comments straight away. Customers are more likely to respond to an interviewer, either on the phone or in person, than to a postal survey.

Achieving a standardised and objective approach can be difficult, but is essential if you wish to gather top quality information. The best way of doing this is to design the interview questions around the standards that have been defined by customers and to train all interviewers carefully.

All these types of measurement systems can provide valuable information that will help you to identify and solve problems and retain customers. But to get the best out of them, you have to monitor them carefully and be prepared to change

your approach if they are not yielding the information you
need.

Using measurement results

The information you collect can tell you about any slippage
or failures before full scale disaster occurs and you can then
take immediate action to rectify the situation. If the results
are good, it is highly motivating for staff to get positive
feedback for their efforts.

Once you have the customer data, you will need to:

- **Analyse it**: it is useful to plot raw data on bar charts or line
  graphs. This will help you to track results over a long
  period of time so that you can obtain a wider picture of
  performance and identify the results of any changes in
  ways of working.

- **Identify any problems or trends**: it is vital not to take the data you have collected at face value. You can get a wider perspective by looking at your findings in conjunction with information from other sources and by talking problems though with colleagues and team members.

- **Communicate the information throughout the organisation**: making the facts widely available shows that you are serious about identifying problems and encourage everyone to take action to improve things. If you display trends and results graphically, employees can quickly see how they are doing in relation to the specified standards and this in itself should motivate them to improve things.

Today's chapter has investigated the things that are important to customers – a crucial element of maintaining their loyalty. Remember that all your customers have requirements from you, and that meeting these requirements is essential if you are to retain them.

Mobilising employees to give customers what they want

In the last chapter we looked at various ways of finding out what customers want and of measuring our success in giving this to them. But customer retention is largely a function of human commitment, and no matter how sophisticated our systems and procedures are, they will only work if employees want to make them work. We have no hope of achieving our customer-defined standards if we don't have the commitment of the entire workforce.

This is why we need to make sure that employees are motivated – that they know what the organisation is about and where it is going, and that they share these goals and want to become involved in achieving them.

Satisfied employees equal satisfied customers

A company director said recently, 'It is difficult to make sure that we deliver customer satisfaction when our relationships with our customers are in the hands of our lowest-paid and least important people'. But how can it be true that the frontline staff are the least important? These staff are the ones with whom the reputation of most companies rests – so they should be seen as the most important.

Employees with the right attitudes are the vital resource that enable successful organisations to translate customer retention concepts into reality. We have to ensure that we hire, train, manage and reward people so that they will enthusiastically carry out the things that are necessary to satisfy the customer. Many organisations now use psychometric tests when selecting staff to pick out people-orientated individuals who actually get a buzz out of dealing with customers.

The first major study to reveal that happy and committed employees lead to happy and loyal customers was done in the early 1990s by Sears Roebuck in the United States. Sears, which had been one of America's largest and most popular retailers, had been slowly drifting downhill. The company started a major reorganisation of staff, with heavy emphasis on training and incentives, trying to make them understand their own importance in saving the stores. It worked – and a net loss of $3.9 billion dollars in 1992 was turned into an enormous profit in the space of just five years.

In the course of rethinking what the company was and what it wanted to become, Sears' managers developed a business model which tracked success from management behaviour through employee attitudes to customer satisfaction and financial performance. Here is a simplified version of the model they developed.

Increased employee satisfaction and loyalty – leads to

Higher quality services and products – leads to

Increased profits and growth – leads to

Increased customer satisfaction and loyalty – leads to

The work of creating the model and associated measures made such demands on the managers involved that it completely changed the way they thought and behaved. They began to see that employee attitudes influenced not just customer service but also employee turnover, organisational performance and, ultimately, profits.

In the first major UK survey of its type, the Institute of Employment Studies looked at the staff attitudes in a large grocery chain. The main finding of the research was that, in stores where staff satisfaction levels were high, sales were significantly higher. It particular, it revealed a clear link between levels of absenteeism and profits. And line managers who were seen to take a supportive attitude on personal matters, were fair, gave feedback and helped to provide career development opportunities also achieved larger turnovers and greater profits.

Although many firms put an enormous effort into trying to get their employees to empathise with their customers and to give good service, the really successful ones have found that it's no good trying to 'robot' people into a particular way of behaving with customers. Only one thing will ensure that people find the right way of doing things for themselves: motivation.

'It's no good telling someone to say Three Bags Full, and smile,' says David Freemantle of Superboss Ltd, 'only motivated staff will find the right way of doing things. Much of the relationship with customers is non-verbal anyway. Stance, and the amount of eye-contact (too little indicates shyness, too much, aggression) can't be written down in a set of rules.'

'We just tell our staff that they should treat the customer as they would wish to be served,' says Craig Williams of John Lewis, where the famously helpful staff are all members of the company co-op and share in its profits. 'We don't need to tell them to whistle and hop.'

From 'Service with a Smile' The Guardian: 27 October 1999

Motivation

This short book is not the place to discuss the psychology of motivation in great detail. But there is space to look at a few practical points that may help you to generate commitment amongst members of your team.

The problem with motivation is that it is an internal drive, so you can't 'motivate' someone else; they can only do this for themselves. All you can do is arrange things – build the structures, produce the systems, create an environment, develop relationships – which will enable people to feel motivated.

To achieve a motivating climate, you have to take into account the various factors that drive individuals. As long ago as 1970, two researchers called Otto and Glaser analysed motivation at work in terms of the rewards that people can achieve. This is how they broke it down.

Motivation	Reward
Achievement	Success
Anxiety	Avoidance of failure
Approval	Gaining the admiration and respect of others
Curiosity	Learning new things
Acquisitiveness	Money and other material benefits

These motivating factors seldom act in isolation, and most people will be motivated by most of them at some time or another. This knowledge provides lots of clues about the right way to treat employees so that they will feel satisfied at work and will, in turn, strive to satisfy customers:

- Team members who are motivated by a desire to achieve must be able to experience success in terms of satisfying and retaining customers. This means setting performance standards, supporting people as they strive to achieve these targets, and praising them when they have been successful.
- People who are motivated primarily by anxiety will need constant reassurance and a lot of positive feedback to give them the confidence in creating positive relationships with customers and in taking personal responsibility.
- Team members who are driven by the desire for approval will need to know that you recognise their experience and their strengths. Again, even the smallest achievement will require plenty of positive feedback and praise.
- You can harness people's curiosity by encouraging them to find things out for themselves – perhaps by interviewing customers, researching new developments or joining project teams.
- As most people are motivated by acquisitiveness, emphasise the fact that retaining customers will improve profitability and, in turn, the prospects of promotion, higher salaries and other material rewards.

A lot of this comes down to building healthy, productive working relationships with the people in your team, valuing them and treating them with respect. In short, you should behave towards team members in the same way that you want them to behave towards customers.

Positive reinforcement
A good way of encouraging appropriate behaviour is to practise positive reinforcement. This is the opposite of criticism and punishment, and involves praising people for

what they do right rather than criticising them for their mistakes and shortcomings. Psychologists who favour positive reinforcement believe that we depend far too heavily on punishment to bring about behavioural change. They argue that positive reinforcement encourages appropriate behaviour and at the same time subtly discourages inappropriate behaviour.

In a business context, positive reinforcement is usually given in the form of feedback and appraisals. The companies that produce the best results, the ones that succeed in making their workforce feel more committed, are those that make an effort to provide positive feedback consistently and regularly.

Appraising individual performance

Because the term 'assessment' carries the connotation of tests and exams, performance assessment is usually now called 'individual appraisal' or 'performance appraisal'. Although many people find the idea daunting, an open assessment policy is essential for developing and maintaining people's enthusiasm and commitment and for ensuring the long-term success of an organisation. Regular, fair appraisal can help people to perform at their best and can increase individuals' sense of security and trust. Quite simply, people do find it motivating to know what others think of their performance. In the context of customer retention, appraisal is the starting point for identifying how attitudes and skills need to be developed to ensure that customers are receiving the right kinds of service.

Successful companies like Virgin, Carphone Warehouse, TNT and Pret à Manger are all now highly focused on motivating their staff with constant assessments and feedback. If your organisation has a high rate of customer or employee turnover, you may need to consider how this might be improved by a structured appraisal programme.

There are several points to bear in mind when planning an appraisal scheme:

- You must introduce the scheme clearly, so that employees know what will be involved and do not become anxious.
- It must be open, so that employees know what criteria are being used for assessment. It's important that people are appraised both on how effectively they carry out their work tasks and on how effectively they contribute to customer retention.
- The scheme should cover all employees – not just those on the front line.
- You should encourage self-assessment – in which people

comment on their own performance and development
needs.
- Appraisal must be regular – probably every six months or
  every year.
- It's important to commit to a system that you know you
  can implement. There is nothing worse than launching a
  scheme in a blaze of publicity and then allowing it to fizzle
  out because of lack of time or commitment.

This is an example of an appraisal form which can be used as
the basis of discussion during an appraisal interview. It is a
good idea for both manager and team members to think
about the questions on the form before the interview.

Name

Post

Department

What part of your work has given you the most
satisfaction over the past year?

What part of your work has give you the least
satisfaction over the past year?

List your major achievements during the year

What skills have you learned or developed?

What would help you to be more efficient in your work?

List your targets for next year

List anything that you need to help you achieve your
targets

The results of such assessments could be the basis for the discussion of an employee's present performance and future possibilities and targets. At the end of the interview you should aim to achieve:

- Agreement on the appraisee's current performance (including a clarification of any areas where there are differences of interpretation)
- Agreement on any training and development needs and how these will be met.

Appraisals should be seen as a constructive review meeting between manager and employee, in which they discuss what has happened in the past and agree future developments. Appraisals are bound to fail if they are simply an opportunity for a manager to tick someone off.

Retaining employees

To retain customers, we need highly motivated, well trained employees. This means that retaining these employees, and their valuable skills knowledge and experience, must be a key element of any retention strategy. If these individuals leave, the business loses an essential element of 'intellectual capital' – and the loss is made even more serious if that person goes to work for a competitor. The company then faces both the difficulty and the cost of finding a replacement.

For all these reasons it is crucial to find out why people leave and how to make them more inclined to stay. While there are many reasons for staff turnover, there is clear evidence that poor relationships with managers are often a major

motivation for leaving. In simple terms, employees leave managers – not companies.

In one large retail chain, for example, one in six employees stated that the most disliked aspect of their job was their manager.

Developing productive relationships with team members
The traditional way of managing has emphasised the control and direction of people and the maintenance of discipline. Such managers have a profound effect on the way team members behave. Rather than focusing on improving services or getting closer to customer's needs, their primary objectives tend to be pleasing the boss and keeping out of trouble.

Research shows that managers who take a positive view of others and encourage responsibility have fewer staff problems than those who believe that that people must be controlled and threatened with punishment before they will make any sort of effort.

By creating positive, open relationships with members of your team, you can do a lot to create the kind of climate where people will want to build similar kinds of relationships with customers. Whatever you decide to do in practical terms, it is vital to model the behaviours that you want others to adopt. For example:

- If you want them to take responsibility – you will have to trust them
- If you want them to be courteous to customers – you will have to treat them with respect
- If you want them to fulfil their promises to customers – you will have to prove yourself to be reliable in everything you do
- If you want them to be innovative in their dealings with customers – you will have to allow them to take risks
- If you want them to be effective – you will have to help them to develop the right skills
- If you want them to be open – you will have to be honest and sincere yourself.

Your example will reinforce the habits you want to enforce and help weed out the ones you want to eliminate.

Today we have looked at some of the key principles that will enable employees to play their part in retaining customers. Encouraging the right attitudes involves first hiring people who like people, and then training, managing and rewarding them to make sure that they remain continually committed to the central goal of delivering customer satisfaction.

Getting better all the time

By now you will have recognised that the aim of satisfying and retaining customers is a moving target because customer requirements are changing all the time and new issues are constantly emerging. It's no good making our products and processes as good as possible and then forgetting about it. To keep ahead of the competition we have to make improving things a way of life.

If you need to be convinced about the value of continuous improvement, think of what the consequences would be for your business if you were still trying to offer the same products and standards of service that you provided 10 or 15 years ago. It is a dangerous strategy – and has been, for the many flagship companies now extinct, a fatal one – to assume that because customers are loyal at the moment they will continue to be so.

Today we look at how you can take a planned approach to continuous improvement.

Why is continuous improvement important?

Very few businesses remain untouched by change. To prosper, we have to respond quickly to changing customer requirements, new competition and advances in technology. We also have to act swiftly to identify and solve any problems that are making customers go elsewhere.

It is important to be aware that the improvements you introduce don't always have to be ambitious. Even apparently modest changes can have a far reaching effect in the way that customers perceive you, in how employees feel and in the results you achieve.

The improvement process

There are four key stages to continuous improvement. Showing them as a cycle underlines the fact that the process is continuous; no sooner have you implemented one activity than it is time to start identifying opportunities for further improvements.

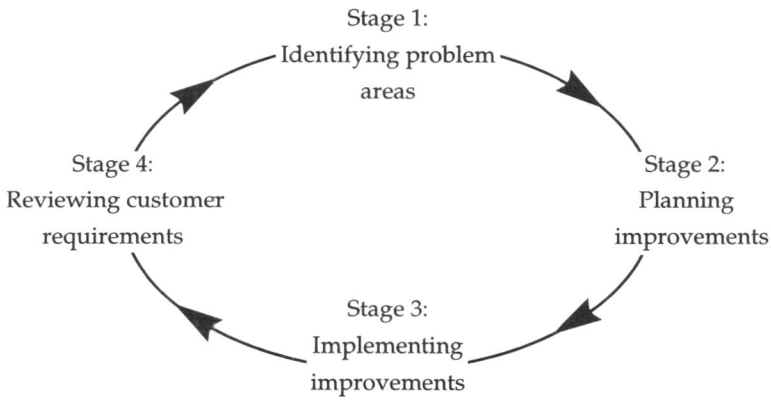

Stage 1:
Identifying problem
areas

Stage 2:
Planning
improvements

Stage 3:
Implementing
improvements

Stage 4:
Reviewing customer
requirements

The type and scale of problem that you identify will determine who becomes involved in planning and implementing the improvement and the techniques to use. However, the basic cycle is the same for all types of problem.

1 Identifying problem areas
The starting point is to identify your customers and their requirements and to assess whether or not these are being met. We covered this stage of the cycle on Monday and Tuesday. If you discover many issues, you will need to find some way of prioritising them so that you can tackle one problem at a time, rather than trying to do everything at once.

2. Planning improvements
This list explains the four basic types of improvement activity that you may be involved in planning:

1 **Responding**: reacting to a problem – putting mistakes right or reworking
2 **Preventing**: learning from experience to ensure that mistakes never happen again
3 **Innovating**: introducing a completely new way of doing things
4 **Creating**: making new opportunities – usually by anticipating customers' needs and adapting processes or products to meet those needs.

As you can see, some types of improvement are introduced merely as a reaction to problems, while others are designed to make the most of new opportunities. Unfortunately, many people spend too much time reacting to problems and crises. Although most will agree how important planning is, many complain that they don't have the time to plan or that things are changing too fast to plan ahead. The message is clear and simple – proactive planning is vital if customer requirements are to be met and customers are to remain loyal.

3   Implementing

As with any plan, the next stage is to try it out. Bear in mind that any changes need to be carefully monitored because there may be unenvisaged knock-on effects, or the plan simply may not work and should be abandoned at the earliest opportunity.

4   Reviewing

Once information has fed back through the process of monitoring, you should review what has happened and ask yourself if it has resulted in improved customer satisfaction. Has your plan improved the service you provide for your customer in the way you anticipated? It's not just the end results that you need to look at – it is also important to review how you achieved them. As part of your review, you also need to find out if the improvement activity selected was actually the most effective for the circumstances.

Experience suggests that the full involvement of the people who have implemented the improvement activity both improves the quality of review and increases commitment to actions agreed as a result.

It's pointless doing a review unless you are going to make good use of your findings. The results of the review session should help you to:

- Improve the way you collect, analyse and communicate measurement information
- Refine your improvement activity process

- Identify areas where you should plan to introduce further
  quality improvements.

Managing change

By definition, improvement implies change. Change,
however, often unsettles people and makes them
uncomfortable. It affects them both individually and as a
group because it threatens to replace existing and known
ways of working with the new and the unknown. A vital
aspect of your role as a manager is to create a climate in
which everyone wants to become positively involved in the
process of change.

The best way to view change is as a new challenge,
something that will motivate people and bring about a better
future. Planned change is for a purpose; for example,
improving efficiency, increasing customer satisfaction or
achieving a larger market share. It can therefore mean more
security and enhanced prospects for individuals, with the
possibility of a higher salary, more enjoyment and more
responsibility.

Involving people
You will find that changes occur smoothly and successfully if
you are able to communicate with team members and
involve them closely in everything that is going on. It is
particularly valuable to discuss with them how changes can
also be opportunities to gain experience and develop new
skills. If you take all the decisions in isolation, employees will
not feel that improvement is their responsibility.

Involving as many people as possible will ensure that you

have all available information and data. The people doing the job at the front end often have some simple and powerful solutions to offer, if only someone would ask them. In addition, a problem shared by the team and a solution reached by the team commands a far greater level of commitment and support than one imposed by a manager. Team members begin to look for ways of making it work rather than identifying self-fulfilling prophesies about why it won't.

In managing the change process, there are some approaches that can help to secure and maintain commitment and deliver the objective you require:

- Provide help and support to those who want it
- Avoid over-organising – let others come up with the ideas and even the plans
- Communicate properly – including listening and answering questions honestly
- Explore the positive and the negative effects of change – and focus on the positive

Every organisation that has tackled the issue of continuous improvement successfully has found that people are the most important resource and that if they are not involved it just doesn't happen.

Tools for implementing continuous improvements

We finish today by summarising some of the tools that many companies have found valuable in identifying problems and improving customers' satisfaction.

- **Brainstorming**: a group technique for generating long lists of ideas and issues
- **Clustering**: a tool for sorting large quantities of unorganised information into groups
- **Force Field Analysis**: a tool for drawing out the factors that restrain progress and the factors that can help to drive it forward
- **Influence circles**: a tool for identifying factors over which you have some control
- **Decision making techniques**: to help you decide which one of a number of issues should take priority
- **Fishbone diagram**: a technique for identifying the many possible causes of a problem and how each cause contributes to the problem
- **Benchmarking**: a process for measuring what we do against our competitors or industry leaders.

Brainstorming

Brainstorming provides an opportunity for a small group of colleagues or members of a team to work together on customer retention issues. It is a means of drawing out a large number of ideas in a short time and is a powerful technique for encouraging people to bounce suggestions off each other and to think creatively, rather than logically.

Brainstorming sessions need to be dynamic, so they should be kept short – ideally no longer than fifteen minutes. You can brainstorm either freely, with people contributing spontaneously, or by taking one idea from each group member in turn. Encourage creative, wild, and seemingly ridiculous notions. For the technique to work, it is vital that group members should never criticise or judge ideas and suggestions. At the end of the session, however, you will need to go through the list of ideas and eliminate duplication, unimportant issues and proposals that are clearly impossible. You will end up with a full list of the customer retention issues or problems that you want to develop further.

Clustering

Clustering will help you to deal with large quantities of unorganised information, for example the ideas thrown up in a brainstorming session. Ideas are categorised into groups and each group is then evaluated separately. The best way to cluster ideas is to write each one on a separate post-it note and to stick them all on a whiteboard or a wall. The most useful categories will become clear as you start the grouping process. Finally, assign headings to the various clusters that you have identified.

The advantage of clustering is that it gives you an opportunity to eliminate or combine duplicated ideas. It may help you to see patterns or trends emerging which may assist in understanding a problem and working towards a solution.

Force Field Analysis

It's best to use this tool when participants have narrowed their thoughts down to one or two that may be workable. A Force Field Analysis will help you to develop an action plan because it draws out the factors that restrain progress and the factors that can help to drive it forward. Here is an example of a 'force field' that could be drawn up around the issue of improving customer retention.

Driving forces	Improving customer retention	Restraining forces
• Good team spirit ➡		⬅ • Low budget
• We want to get involved		• Little time
• Fear of unemployment		• Lack of confidence
• Boss is on our side		• Skills deficit

Once group members have identified the different elements that may help or hinder success, they can develop action steps that build on the driving forces and reduce the restraining forces.

Influence circles

When trying to plan improvements it is all too easy to get bogged down in seemingly insurmountable problems like low budgets, bad managers, legal issues or lack of time. But in reality there are always some factors which can be changed, although there are also many more which cannot be overcome.

'Influence circles' are a way of identifying the areas which you can control.

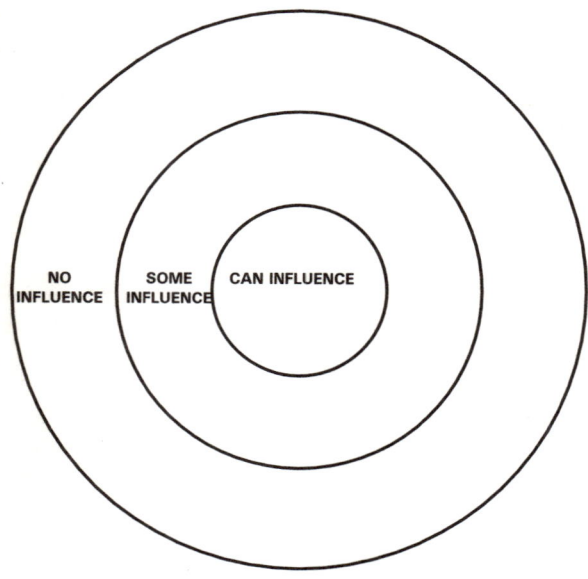

NO INFLUENCE   SOME INFLUENCE   CAN INFLUENCE

To use the influence circles, you simply place issues or problems in the appropriate part of the diagram – then you focus your action planning around the ones which appear in the central and middle circles.

Be aware that some problems may not be quite so insoluble as they may at first appear. Through discussion, you may be able to convince team members that some issues can be placed in the central and middle circles – rather than in the outer one.

Decision-making techniques

You can use a number of techniques to help choose which one of a number of customer retention problems or solutions merits further time and attention. Three common ones are consensus, voting and negotiation:

- **Consensus**: to reach a consensus you have to keep the discussion going until you arrive at an agreed decision. To make this approach work, everyone must be honest about their true opinions and all participants must have a chance to say what they think.

- **Voting**: this method is widely used when it is difficult to reach a consensus. You should only use it if everyone present is prepared to be committed to the outcome of the vote.

- **Negotiation**: this is a way of arriving at a compromise – it can be used when parties who hold opposing views have to come to a decision that is mutually acceptable. The aim of negotiation is to ensure that everyone gets some element of what they want.

Fishbone diagrams

Fishbone diagrams are used to present complex issues or problems and to help identify how a variety of causes contributes to a particular problem or outcome.

If you were trying to analyse the reasons why customers are defecting to the competition, you might draw a fishbone diagram as follows:

1 List all the possible causes (you could do a brainstorm)
2 Group the causes together under headings (you could use clustering to categorise them)
3 Draw a horizontal line with an arrow pointing towards the problem
4 For each heading, draw a line off the main line (like a fish skeleton) and write the heading at the end of it.

This is what the fishbone diagram might look like:

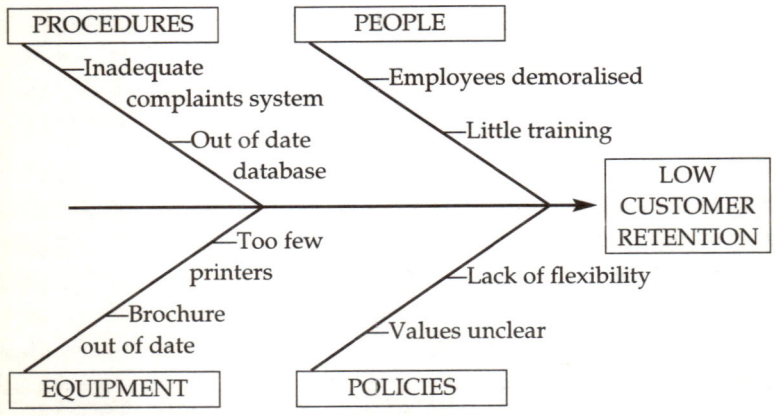

Fishbone diagrams are useful for:

- Exploring the root causes and effects of a problem
- Sorting and displaying causes

- Identifying how causes relate to each other
- Presenting information graphically.

Benchmarking

Benchmarking – taking the absolute best as a standard and then trying to equal it or surpass it – is a key part of any organisation's customer retention strategy. Basically it involves identifying practices from other organisations that you would like to copy. You can improve all business processes by understanding, adapting and adopting the things that others do, and it's often used as a way of improving customer retention.

Inexperienced benchmarkers often make the mistake of looking only at practices that occur within their own industry. Others believe that they have to benchmark with their competitors. If that's all the benchmarking you do, you'll be missing out on valuable opportunities to learn from the good practices of a range of companies..

Many business processes are common in a number of industries. For example, a hospital and a hotel have similar catering and laundry operations. A higher education institution has the same human resource requirements as a civil service department. And a phone company needs the same customer service skills as an insurance broker. The more creative you can be when selecting a company to benchmark with, the more you will be able to learn. It's sometimes called 'moving outside the frame'.

Benchmarking involves four basic steps:

1 Clarify what you are doing to retain customers.

2 Analyse what high performing companies are doing to

retain their customers.

3 Compare your own performance with that of others analysed.

4 Finally, implement the steps necessary to close the performance gap.

Although direct contact with the organisations being benchmarked is the ideal, this is not always possible in practice. You can gather much useful information indirectly from industry contacts, technical journals, trade publications, advertisements, annual reports and from customers.

Benchmarking was originally developed by manufacturing companies but recently many organisations in the service sector have also discovered the value of this tool in satisfying and retaining customers.

Retaining customers when things go wrong

No one likes to deal with complaints. It can be hard work or upsetting to handle customers who are difficult or angry, and it is often time consuming to put the matter right. Yet if we pay full attention to the complaints we receive, we will prosper. There are two reasons for this:

- If someone is complaining it means we haven't satisfied them yet – and we need to know why
- We are also getting a wonderful opportunity to delight the customer in the way that we resolve the problem.

Today you will explore some guidelines for dealing with dissatisfied customers and turning failures into golden opportunities to delight customers and ensure that they remain loyal.

This poster is displayed in one organisation with a strong commitment to retaining customers:

Rule 1: The customer is always right

Rule 2: When the customer is wrong, return to Rule 1.

Why you should encourage complaints

When things go wrong, the customer is presented with a good reason to switch providers and to tell others to not use the service. Effective recovery is therefore essential to save and even build the relationship with that customer. If the organisation fails in recovery, it has failed the customer twice

– a double deviation from customer expectations.

Studies have shown that more than 90% of dissatisfied customers don't complain – they simply go elsewhere next time they want to buy. This means that many of us could be deluding ourselves that our customers are happy with the services or products that we provide. Furthermore, for every complaint we actually receive, there are several other customers with problems – some of which could be serious.

If you think that these facts are hard to believe, consider your own experience as a customer. How many times have you been rather less than happy with a meal served in a restaurant, the length of time you have had to wait in a doctor's surgery, the way a shop assistant spoke to you or the after-sales service on a computer. And how often have you actually complained?

There are many reasons why people don't complain:

- They can't be bothered
- They don't want to cause a fuss

- They think that complaining won't do any good
- They don't know how to complain or who to complain to.

Interestingly, research shows that dissatisfied non-complainers are the people who are least likely to be repeat buyers. Even a customer who is not satisfied with the way you responded to a complaint is more likely to buy again than someone who does not complain at all. It follows that a massive percentage of unhappy customers will defect to the competition – and you will not even know that they are dissatisfied, let alone the reason for their dissatisfaction.

Although dissatisfied customers may not complain to you, they still feel frustrated and aggrieved and they want to let off steam. Typically, they will complain to any number of other customers and potential customers about their poor experiences (surveys suggest that dissatisfied customers tell around 12 people about the way they feel, while satisfied customers pass the good news on to only three people). The potential for damage to a business is even greater now in the age of the world wide web. Now, disgruntled customers can post their poor experiences online or e-mail their complaints to thousands of other potential buyers in a matter of seconds.

In this complex and overcrowded market place, where many customers buy on the recommendations of their friends and acquaintances, such negative word-of-mouth advertising can be extremely harmful.

However, the good news is that many benefits emerge if you make it easy for people to complain and if you deal with their complaints satisfactorily. By encouraging people to complain and then resolving their problems quickly and effectively:

- You keep existing customers
- You develop your relationships with them
- Those customers are likely to win you more customers because they will go and tell friends how impressed they were with you
- The original complaint itself becomes unimportant!

If, on the other hand, you make it hard for people to complain, you will not only lose the dissatisfied customers; you will also lose potential customers who hear about the failure second-hand.

By making it easy for people to communicate their dissatisfaction you can quickly build up a picture which will help to avoid similar problems in the future. You can also make sure that what you are offering is what people actually want – rather than what you think they want.

Empowering the front line to take care of complaints

There is nothing like a well-handled complaint for satisfying customers and making them want to come back. You only have to think of your own experience as a customer if, as the result of a complaint, the organisation concerned put things right speedily and with good grace.

Unfortunately, what often happens is that the front line employees who receive complaints take them personally. As a result, they over-react and become defensive. To overcome this kind of reaction, it can help to think of the complaint as a genuine wish to solve the problem by someone who has taken the time and the trouble to visit, write or telephone.

Whenever possible, the complaint taker should grasp the initiative and seek to deal with the complaint on the spot. This looks better than having to call in a manager or supervisor to sort things out. Most people are quite capable of handling complaints effectively – and it is better for the organisation's image if everyone is prepared to do this. In addition, there is nothing more annoying to a customer than having to explain the nature of a problem to a succession of different people as he or she is passed from one extension to another.

Very often, all the customer really wants is an acknowledgement of the problem, an apology, an explanation and a solution to the problem. The solutions offered could be:

- **A refund**: shops, mail order companies and online retailers can build customer loyalty by refunding or trading in defective goods, no questions asked

- **An upgrade**: for example airlines, car hire firms or hotels provide customers with better seats, better cars or better rooms at the same price when the original reservation is not available.

A process for handling complaints

If they want to be effective at handling complaints, team members have to be flexible because each customer and each set of circumstances is unique. Nevertheless, all complaints should be dealt with systematically. Encourage your staff always to look on the positive side by being pleased that they have been given the opportunity to correct a mistake, rather than losing an customer and damaging the company's image

In this extract from their book about BT's drive to transform itself by putting customers first, Johnson and Jakeman describe the importance of 'the psychological angle' when dealing with complaints.

The way we handle complaints can make the difference between a customer with a minor gripe and a customer who is livid.

One of the most important things is to look at the problem from the customer's point of view. This means taking the customer very seriously – letting them know that their problem is important to us. People are often nervous when they ring in. They think that we won't understand how important it is to them to get the problem fixed. It makes a huge difference simply to let them know that we aren't going to shrug them off, but that we're going to do everything we can to put things right.

Extract from *The Customer Challenge* by Johnson and Jakeman

There are six main stages to handling complaints:

1 **Listen**: aim to diffuse the customer's feelings and clarify the exact nature of the problem
2 **Sympathise**: this means sympathising with the fact that the person has a problem, not accepting any blame
3 **Don't justify, argue or make excuses**: just stick to the facts, keep off what happened in the past and focus on what is going to happen now
4 **Ask questions**: this will give you more detailed information about the specific complaint and allow you to see a way through to a possible solution to the problem
5 **Agree a course of action**: it is essential to find a solution which is satisfactory for the customer and from your organisation's point of view
6 **Check the course of action is carried out**: if you agree with the customer that something will happen by a certain date, you must check that it has in fact happened. If it hasn't, you must take action to avoid making the problem even more serious.

A builder's merchant failed to deliver a consignment of materials on the agreed date. The customer contacted the sales office and was told that scheduling difficulties were responsible. The drop was arranged for the following day – but again did not materialise. When the customer rang again, the reason given for the second failure was that a driver had left at short notice. Although these problems may in themselves have been unavoidable, the combined result of two delivery failures with no communication to the client was both the loss of a long-standing customer and the creation of damaging word-of-mouth negative publicity.

Dealing with angry customers

Nobody has to listen to abuse passively. However, you and your team should not fall into the trap of reacting and matching their angry behaviour so that a heated argument ensues.

Using the following guide will help you to tackle angry customers:

Dealing with anger – Dont's
- Don't get angry yourself
- Don't be defensive
- Don't take it personally
- Don't give a flat 'no' – try to offer alternatives
- Don't pass the customer on to someone else – take personal responsibility for dealing with the situation
- Don't allocate blame – try to solve the problem
- Don't make promises you cannot keep

Dealing with anger – Do's
- Be professional, understanding and patient
- Let the customer 'blow off steam' before attempting to deal with the problem

- Find out and use the customer's name and offer your own name
- Show you care about how the customer feels and do your best to help her/him
- Find out what the problem really is, listen carefully and check your understanding
- Find out what the customer's ideal solution is and discuss how this might be achieved
- Agree an achievable solution or a plan of action and deliver it.

HE NEEDED SOME SPACE TO COOL OFF

Monitoring complaints

Properly compiled complaint data can show how consumers interpret your advertising, how products and services meet (or do not meet) consumer expectations and how consumer information can be improved. This is why it is a good idea to keep full records of complaints. These can be collected regularly, followed up and tabulated so that trends can be identified and analysed.

A well planned system for monitoring complaint data can provide answers to important questions, such as:

- How many complaints?
- What was the nature of the complaints?
- How many were justified?
- Which complaints were product-centred and which were person-centred (material service or personal service)?
- What are the proposed remedial actions?
- What are customers' attitudes after the complaint has been handled?

Complaints should be recorded systematically in an appropriate place, so that everyone can learn from them and trends or recurring problems can be spotted before too much damage has been done.

Staff in a GP surgery monitored patients' complaints and found that many of them concerned the behaviour of staff in the reception area. It immediately used training to improve their interpersonal skills – and complaints soon dropped by nearly two thirds.

Learning to love complaints

We all know that dealing with complaints can be very difficult and very time consuming – but we need to welcome them because they are an honest guide to how customers see us. Taking a positive attitude towards complaints and learning from them is a vital part of improving our service and finding out how to give our customers what they want.

Remember, a customer who complains is in fact giving us a

second a chance. This is why we should welcome complaints. He or she could have just 'voted with their feet' – and we would not have had the chance to regain a lost customer.

By complaining, customers are giving us an opportunity to:

- Find out what we need to do to improve our systems and procedures
- Identify areas where we need to train our staff
- See our service from the customer's point of view
- Highlight new services which our customers may require from us.

The main point that has emerged today is the importance of changing our attitude towards complaints. We should no longer see them as threats or inconveniences, but rather as insights into what we need to do to make our products and services more attractive for customers.

Rewarding people

The central idea of this book has been that it makes more sense to retain existing customers than to spend a lot of money and effort on finding new ones. This is particularly true for high spending customers – there may be very few of them but they could account for some 80% of your revenue. But even the 'small' customers are important because they might grow into bigger customers or make recommendations to other customers.

The ideas that you will explore today are based on the work of the psychologist Dr Eric Berne who also developed the concept of Transactional Analysis. While studying the psychology of human motivation. Berne noted that people of all ages may develop mental disorders if they are deprived of human contact. Because people have a basic need to be recognised, they will be happier and more motivated if other human beings pay attention to them and show that they value them.

Berne coined the word 'stroke' to describe a single unit of acknowledgement (which could take the form of simply remembering someone's name or sayng hello) and argued that people simply can't survive without 'strokes'. It follows that if your organisation is not geared up to provide staff and customers with appropriate 'strokes' they will go somewhere else to get them. Providing appropriate personal recognition to both these groups is a simple way of improving staff performance and customer retention.

Rewarding customers from the start

To give customers the right first impression and to ensure that they keep coming back, you need to start building their loyalty right from the first moment they contact you or come through the door. It doesn't matter whether they are placing an order worth several thousand pounds or are merely contacting your company with a request for information, every one of them must be made to feel appreciated and valued.

Rewarding customers does not automatically involve giving everyone prizes – although providing discounts or gifts is one way of getting new customers to commit themselves. Almost more important are the inexpensive rewards like remembering people's names, showing an interest and a simple 'thank you for calling us'. None of this has to be cloying or artificial – the aim must be to be as natural and friendly as possible. It's just a question of real sincerity and ordinary good manners.

Such small civilities seem almost too obvious to mention, but in reality they are very powerful strokes because they tell customers that they have made an impression on you, that you respect them and that they are important. Customers appreciate these kinds of rewards because they are like subtle compliments – and everyone likes to feel appreciated or admired. One study showed that two thirds of customers who stop doing business with companies do so because those companies neglect them or treat them indifferently.

To get an idea of what it feels like from a customers' point of view, consider the warm feeling you get when someone in a shop or on the end of the phone remembers who you are or takes an interest in serving you. Then think of the number of times you have bought something without anyone even bothering to speak to you or acknowledge you in the smallest way. Which companies would you rather do business with a second time?

Convince customers that you value them by encouraging everyone to use appropriate words and body language. Try the following – not necessarily in this order:

- Thank them for doing business with you
- Make eye contact
- Smile
- Greet them
- Use their names
- Shake hands, if appropriate.

It is just as important (and probably more important) to use an appropriate version of these concepts when you are doing business over the telephone or online. Technology makes it possible to create the right impression with many thousands of customers very cheaply. A polite, fast acknowledgement of an order by e-mail is reassuring for customers and makes them feel that their business is valued. And when an order has been fulfilled, the occasional newsletter or (increasingly) e-letter are a great way to stay in touch with customers, to introduce new products and services, to celebrate successes and to say thanks to them for doing business with you.

Convincing them you care

Although positive words and body language are powerful tools in the battle to persuade customers that they are valued and that we want to retain them, there are many situations in which we need to make a stronger and more lasting impression. In these cases it can be useful to provide customers with more tangible 'strokes'.

Here are some examples of the variety of small ways in which companies reward old and new customers and encourage them to come back:

- A motor service and repairs company sends tasteful cards to all new customers thanking them for trusting the company to work on their cars and assuring them of their best attention
- On the final day of their stay in a Spanish Parador, guests receive a folder of tinted engravings as a farewell gift and a reminder of their visit
- On its 10th anniversary, a credit card company sent a personalised thank you letter to all its customers, together with a gift of a phone message pad. Customer are reminded of the company's name every time they use the pad
- A publisher offers gift tokens to schools in return for being allowed to put on exhibitions and sell its titles at school events. The schools use the tokens as raffle prizes and the winners buy their books from the publisher
- When first time customers are checking out of a health club, they are given a certificate which offers a 20% discount off normal prices. They can either use the certificate themselves or pass it on to friend – in either case the idea creates repeat business.

If you think that some of these ideas are a pricey way of persuading an existing customer to come back, remember how much it costs to acquire a new customer. One company found that the cost of finding a single new customer was more than the cost of the product.

Just a health warning about these types of approaches, however. They do not generally provide long-term advantages unless they are combined with another strategy. Although financial incentives and other rewards are important to some customers, they can easily be imitated by competitors. No matter how imaginative or tempting a reward programme, it is no compensation for dirty premises, bad pricing or poor service.

Rewarding customers for long-term loyalty

Giving additional or better rewards to customers who remain loyal over an period of time is particularly worthwhile because the longer they stay with you the more profitable they will be. Most companies' revenue tends to follow the Pareto principle – you get about 80% of your income from

20% of your customers. So identify your top 20%, and then treat them so well that they will never consider buying from the competition.

You can consolidate your best customers' loyalty in many different ways; from offering gifts and organising celebrations to creating special services and rewarding high frequency.

Creating special services
Providing 'elite' services for high spending customers is a good way of adding value for them at little extra cost and, at the same time, making them feel special. Examples include:

- Banks which offer 'advantage' programmes (including free insurance for holidays and purchases) for customers whose incomes or sums deposited are above average

- Airlines which offer travellers who fly more than a certain number of miles every year extra services like fast check-in, access to VIP lounges and many other perks

- Hotel chains which make their top customers feel special by giving them things like free upgrades, gifts of flowers and individualised attention

- An evening at the opera or an afternoon at a tennis match can help to strengthen relationships with high spending customers. Such events make even more of impression when the host company is a sponsor.

Rewarding frequency
Businesses often try to bind customers closer to them by offering lower prices for greater volume purchases or rewards for long-term customers. These strategies are called

'frequency programmes' and, again, you don't have to look far to find examples:

- Some hotel chains offer their guests points for each time they stay in any of their hotels, redeemable for room nights, meals or other types of services

- Long-distance telephone companies in the United States provide volume discounts and other price incentives to retain market share and build a loyal customer base

- Frequent callers using the services of New Zealand telephone companies earn points based on their monthly bills which can be cashed in for speciality services like call waiting or phone cards

- Retail chains use loyalty cards to provide points-based rewards for customers who shop frequently with them. The rewards offered range from free gifts to discounts and air miles. A particularly imaginative example is a pet supermarket which offers a free dog bath and grooming service to customers whose cards show that they have made eight visits

- The online business world is brimming with schemes to build traffic and reward frequency. E-companies come up with new schemes all the time – rewards include the chance to enter daily or weekly competitions, receive free samples, access information and make new contacts.

Although some of these strategies may only be possible for very large companies, you can probably think of many creative ways of telling customers that you value them – whatever the size of your organisation.

Rewarding employees

Research confirms that, the more people are recognised and rewarded for the work they do, the more they are willing to extend themselves – both for the organisation and for their own sense of satisfaction in doing a job well.

On Wednesday and Thursday we discussed the contribution that individual employees make to retaining customers. We saw that we need to recruit the right people, make sure that they know what is expected of them and provide them with the skills to perform those tasks. Sometimes this may involve encouraging them to accept new responsibilities, or even to make a journey into unknown territory. If they are to continue in this way and to encourage others to follow them, it is vital to show that you appreciate their efforts and their achievements.

Many companies that have come to realise the value of motivational rewards operate systems such as commission on sales, 'employee of the month' awards and productivity bonuses.

Marriot International Hotels celebrates service excellence with annual awards to employees who regularly bring to life the company's customer service values.

The trouble with these formal systems is that rewards can take a long time to reach those who have earned them and they are often not shared by many of the people who play an important part in building customer loyalty. It is therefore important for managers at all levels to devise their own reward systems and to encourage a climate where everyone (not just those in charge) expresses their appreciation for colleagues' contributions.

The following list shows a range of possible formal and informal recognition and reward activities. Some of these are just common sense and you may already practise them. However, it's surprising how often team leaders and managers forget to show their people just how much they are valued.

- **Taking a personal interest**: this makes others feel valued as individuals and not just 'cogs in a machine'
- **Acknowledgements**: these are a written or verbal expression of thanks or praise for deadlines achieved, targets met or work well done
- **Tangible rewards**: a company or a team leader can show appreciation by giving small rewards like a tray of cakes, a box of chocolates, theatre tickets or vouchers for meals or goods
- **Publicising success**: you can use team meetings, noticeboards, newsletters or newspapers to make

particular achievements public
- **Celebrating success**: impromptu parties and informal gatherings are often just as valuable for acknowledging achievements as the more a formal 'prize-giving' or annual dinner.

One word of warning – although most individuals enjoy having others' attention drawn to their achievements, it is a good idea to check that you will not cause embarrassment.

Giving feedback
Constructive feedback, praise, positive reinforcement, call it what you will, is probably the most valuable 'stroke' you can give your team. The reason is simple – this tells them that you have noticed them, that you have taken an interest in what they are doing, that you value their efforts and that you think they have potential for doing even better. Feedback is particularly important in the context of customer retention because it reinforces the right kind of behaviour and discourages the attitudes that make customers defect to the competition.

Managers have always given their staff feedback – but if you give in a constructive way it shows people that you recognise the extent and nature of people's role in retaining customers and achieving business success. Feedback motivates individuals in a number of important ways:

- It leaves them in no doubt about what is expected of them, and how they match up to these expectations
- It allows them to understand where their strengths are and the areas where there may be room for improvement
- It tells them that you care about what they are doing and are ready to offer all kinds of help and support

- It underlines the importance of their work in the context of the wider organisation.

Given the potential of feedback to increase motivation, it may be surprising to learn that many business leaders either forget to give it, are embarrassed to give it or do not think that it is important.

Guidelines for feedback
To give feedback effectively, it is important to be aware of these guidelines:

- **Be clear about what you want to say**: try to take a few breaths and gather your thoughts for a moment before speaking

- **Be positive**: if you prove that you recognise and value their positive points, people are more likely to act on the negative ones
- **Be specific**: it does not matter whether you are offering

positive or negative feedback, both should be specific statements relating to a person's work or behaviour
- **Offer alternatives**: it's often useful to come up with suggestions as to what someone could do better or differently, rather than simply criticising or giving advice
- **Avoid making value judgements**: simply saying 'That's no good', does not tell a person anything useful. It is more helpful to say exactly why you think something is no good.

Feedback is empowering and motivating because it makes individuals more aware of themselves and brings them face to face with the consequences of their behaviour. But because we are so unused to the openness and honesty that is required during feedback it can be very painful. It is therefore important to apply the above rules strictly if you don't want to destroy a person's self confidence.

You can give feedback in any situation – both in formal one-to-one meetings when you have a particular issue to deal with or informally as and when the need arises. It is also useful to get others to give each other feedback and it is especially valuable to encourage the people you work with to give you feedback.

Dealing with 'difficult' people
It may happen that, in spite of your best efforts, members of your team do not live up to the customer retention standards that you and the organisation require. If this happens, you must spend time with them trying to work out what the problem is, why it is happening and how it can best be solved. Your role is to deal with such situations constructively and in a way that does not damage your longer term relationship with the team and the climate you are trying to create.

Here are some principles which can help you to deal with an employee whose attitudes may be driving customers away:

- Have a meeting with the person and remind them of the organisation's customer retention targets and the importance of his or her role in achieving these
- Explain exactly what you would like them to do, letting them know precisely what standards you want them to achieve
- Actively encourage feedback to your comments and suggestions and listen carefully to what they say. Include any valid suggestions in the strategy you agree
- Show genuine appreciation of the person's work, indicating that you are confident that he or she can meet the standard required
- Offer any coaching and support that may be necessary to help the person to achieve the standard
- Make an appointment to meet again in a few weeks' time to review the strategy and to identify any improvements that have been made. If the standards are still not being met, agree a new action plan.

When the person does achieve the required standard, it is important to recognise this with some form of appropriate reward. If you treat people with respect, even the most difficult team members may surprise you. It's not that they don't want to serve customers or don't have the ability to do it, they simply need the help and support of leaders who are themselves committed to customer retention and understand how to do it. In the end, your appreciation of their efforts is probably their best reward.

And finally . . .

We have spent the week looking at various aspects of a topic few people in any form of organisation can afford to ignore – how to retain existing customers. I hope that you found some ideas that will help you, your team and your organisation to make customers happier. Maybe you'll be building on things you are already doing or be inspired to try something new.

On Sunday you looked at why customer retention has become so important in recent times – it is profitable and the consequences of not taking it seriously can be disastrous. You saw that although moving from product orientation to customer focus can be a painful process, it has many benefits for the organisation, for customers themselves and for individual employees.

On Monday you saw that to retain customers you need to get a clear idea of who they are and what their requirements are. But getting to know them better can be a sizeable task, as you may have many groups of customers, all with different requirements that have to be satisfied.

On Tuesday you identified some of the main factors that most customers look for in a supplier. You also examined some methods for gathering information about their needs and how well you are meeting these.

On Wednesday you saw that your most important resource for retaining customers is a team that is committed to achieving customer defined standards. You looked at some guidelines for ensuring that employees want to be involved in the drive to retain customers.

■■■ A N D F I N A L L Y ■■■

On Thursday you concentrated on the need to keep improving things in order to keep up with customers' changing requirements and the pressure of change in the wider environment. We emphasised the need to involve the team in identifying areas for improvement and putting ideas into practice.

On Friday you recognised that a customer complaint can actually be one of the most valuable tools in your customer retention strategy. Although a failure to meet standards can give the customer an excellent reason for finding another provider, a complaint dealt with effectively is a golden opportunity to delight customers and ensure that they remain loyal.

Finally, today, you looked at using different kinds of rewards to nurture loyalty – both for customers and for members of the team.

Total success in taking care of customers and retaining them is a goal that cannot be attained overnight. Some of your activities will lead to small wins – for you, your team, your organisation and your customers, and it may at times seem that your own contribution is having a limited impact. But by now you should realise that all your achievements will create ripples that affect both customers and other people in other departments. In the often thankless world of the manager, that is worth a lot.

Books

Frazer-Robinson, J., *Building Customer Loyalty*, 1999, David Grant Publishing Ltd.

Furlong Carla B., *Marketing for keeps: building your business by retaining your customers*, 1993, John Wiley & Sons, Inc.

Johnson T. & Jakeman, M., *The Customer Challenge*, 1997, Pitman Publishing.

Peters, T., *Thriving on Chaos*, 1991, Pan Books.

Peters, T. & Austin, N., *A Passion for Excellence*, Fontana/Collins, 1986 (pages 37–112).

Schonberger, R., *Building a Chain of Customers*, 1990, Business Books.

Sheth, J. and Sobel, A., *Clients for Life*, 2001, Simon and Schuster.

Whiteley, R.C., *The Customer Driven Company: Moving from Talk to Action*, 1991, Random House.

SUN

MON

TUE

WED

THU

FRI

SAT

For information

on other

IN A WEEK titles

go to

www.inaweek.co.uk